The Benefits of Working

Geary Reid

ISBN: 978-976-8305-65-7

Acknowledgments

Great thanks must be expressed to the following people:

The heavenly Father, for granting me the wisdom and inspiration to record the information in this book, which I began on October 27, 2021, and completed on October 30, 2021; my family, for their continued encouragement and support regarding various challenges; and several people who have assisted with reviewing and editing the book:

- Wonnette Nicholson, Dipl. in Business Management and Administration
- Helen Browman, Bsc. Soc. Sc., MBA
- Joyce Sullivan

To you, the reader: have fun while reading, and grasp and practice what you learn so that this world will become a better place. Many people are depending on your guidance. We all need a shoulder to lean on and a hand to guide us.

Geary Reid
MBA, FCCA, FAAPM, MPM, CAT

Reid's Learning Institute and Business Consultancy

reidnlearn.com

Amazon: amazon.com/author/gearyreid

Facebook: Reid n Learn

Instagram: Reid n Learn

LinkedIn: Reid's Learning Institute
and Business Consultancy

199 Kuru - Kururu, Soesdyke Linden Highway
Guyana, South America

Table of Contents

Introduction

Working is a big challenge for many persons. Due to the challenges that employees may share with their friends and family, some persons decide that they hate work. Children may see their parents working long hours and make up their minds that they do not want to work with any organization. However, while work will always have its challenges, there are many benefits for those who are employed.

Employees know that as long as they perform their duties for their leaders, they will be compensated at the end of the week or month. Many persons would like to have greater compensation, but they must remember that many other persons do not have any regular flow of income, so they must be thankful for whatever money they receive. This compensation will allow employees to meet their financial needs, and if they use their money wisely, they may be able to construct their own houses, purchase vehicles, or have savings. Those who are working may also receive many other benefits, such as sales commissions, bonuses, medical benefits, various allowances, and long service awards.

When persons are working, they have the opportunity to develop many friendships among employees, customers, suppliers, and representatives from government agencies and the private sector. Besides the friendships that some employees may enjoy, there are opportunities to find companions at the workplace. Many persons may not join an organization looking for a companion, but their quality of work, mannerisms, and lifestyle may cause at least one of their fellow employees to be attracted to them, and thereafter, it is time for marriage and family life.

As persons go through many stresses and family challenges at home, they may seek employment as an escape from their home and family issues. In this case, the money may not be the main reason why they are working, but because they can spend most of their time away from family matters and stress, they consider this a worthwhile incentive for relieving the pressures and monotony of home life.

Those who are working may recognize that they can engage in daily exercise that will keep them in shape and allow them to be healthy. The diet that persons consume must be carefully monitored if they want to remain healthy.

When persons work, they can develop professional skills in many areas. Those whose skills are developed may benefit from an increase in compensation, as they may be promoted because of their knowledge and skills. The workplace can cause many persons to find their talents. Working may also allow persons to be a source of motivation to others, as other persons choose to work because they want to be motivated. From this literature, the reasons why persons choose to work will become clearer to you. So, work hard and smart. Be a great employee and enjoy your benefits.

1. Ability to earn

Being employed does many important things for people, such as providing the ability to earn. While some persons may be comfortable at home since they have enough money to provide for their needs, other persons have to seek employment to meet their financial needs.

1.1 What do employees do with their compensation?

There are many things that persons will do with their compensation from work. As some persons' compensation is small, they will have to carefully manage whatever they receive so that they can survive until the next payday.

Figure 1. Possible uses of salaries and wages

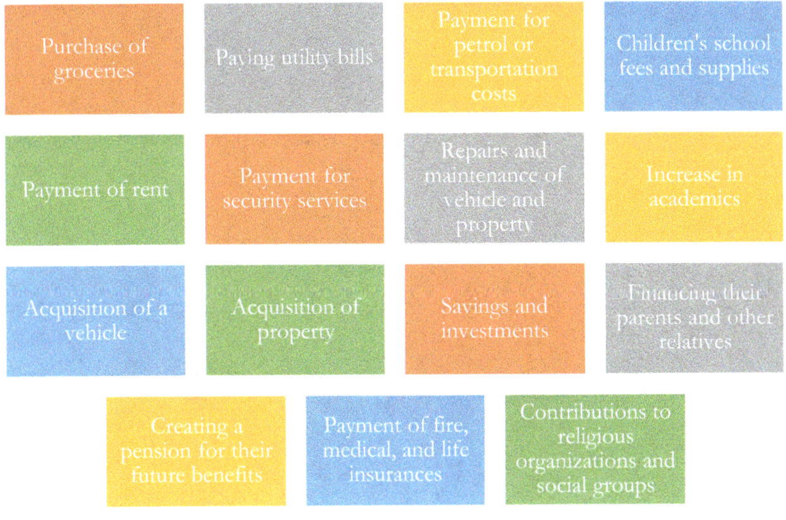

(All figures developed by the author unless otherwise noted.)

1.1.1 Purchase of groceries

Everyone needs to eat, no matter how healthy or spiritual they are. There are times when some religious persons may fast, but after they have fasted, they are required to eat and drink once again. If persons have to visit a medical institution for an inspection or operation, then they may have to go without food and beverages for a specific period. Once they have completed the examination, then they can continue to eat and drink as normal.

The quantity and quality of groceries that persons purchase will be different from others, even if they are earning the same compensation. Most persons like to know that they have enough groceries in their house to last them until the next payday. Some persons can purchase certain groceries in wholesale quantities, so they may have some items that will last them for several weeks.

Those who are working often look forward to their wages and salaries being paid promptly. If there is a delay in their payment, then multiple unpleasant things may happen, as they may have many expenses to settle.

The money that persons receive is often used to meet their physiological needs, according to Maslow's hierarchy of needs (Cole 1993). Food, clothing, and security are the greatest need for many persons. When they work, they set aside money to provide for those needs.

Figure 2. Maslow's hierarchy of needs

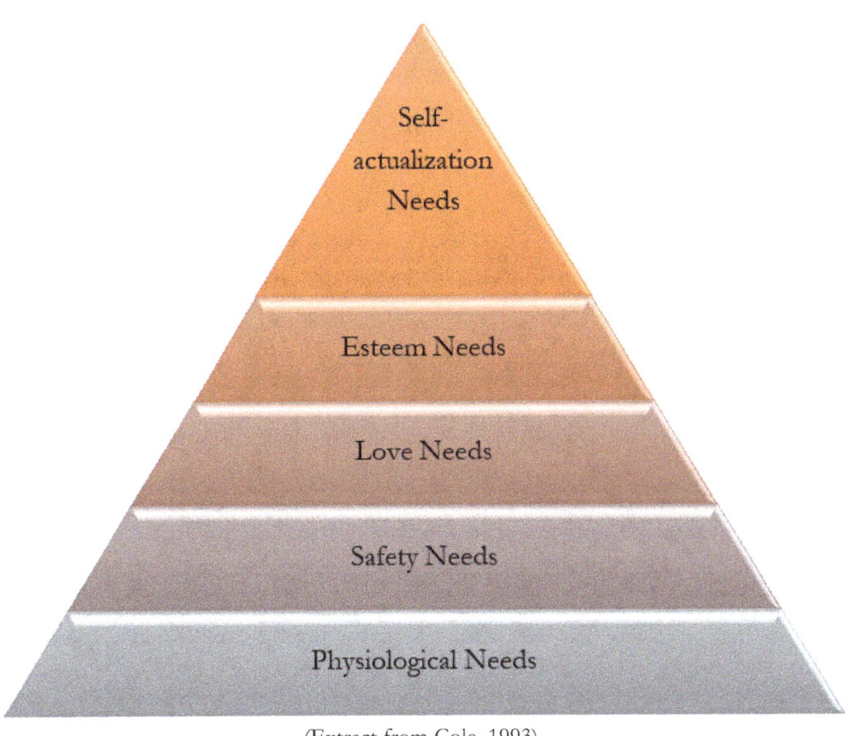

(Extract from Cole, 1993)

After persons' physiological needs are met, then they will venture into putting aside money to meet other needs. Persons who work for longer durations and with greater dedication will have enough money to construct their own house or purchase a vehicle.

1.1.2 Paying utility bills

Employees can apply for vacations, but utility bills will not go on their own vacations. If persons do not want to incur certain utility bills, then they can stop the use of those utility services. However, some utility companies will have a fixed charge that every user of the service must pay. Besides the fixed charge, persons will have to pay for the direct consumption of the utility services within the billing period.

Persons who can afford solar energy will not have to pay utility bills. Their initial investment in solar energy may be high, but after some years, they may fully recover from their initial investment, such that the benefits outweigh the costs.

1.1.3 Payment for petrol or transportation costs

If a person has their own vehicle, they will also have to incur the cost of petrol. There are some employees whose status within the organization may allow them to benefit from a travel allowance, or the organization may pay for the petrol their vehicles use. However, this benefit is often available only to senior employees, while junior employees will have to pay for their petrol.

Those who do not own a vehicle will have to incur transportation costs, which often vary based upon the distance they have to travel. Those who have to travel shorter distances will incur lower transportation costs compared to those who have to travel longer distances. If a person uses a cab for transportation, they may incur higher costs compared to someone who uses public transportation.

1.1.4 Children's school fees and supplies

Not all employees have children. However, some persons seek employment because they have to provide for their children, which includes paying for school fees and supplies. Even when organizations offer scholarships to students, their parents may still have to pay for some basic supplies. Students without full scholarships will have to purchase books and clothes for school.

Some schools may not require fees. However, for many private schools, parents will have to pay school fees. Therefore, some parents will seek employment because they have to pay those school fees regularly. In homes with several school-age children, school fees may be challenging for one parent to afford, so both parents may eventually have to work to pay those fees.

Students may also have lesson fees, and parents will have to earn enough to pay those additional costs. Most parents want their children to be educated, so they will make sacrifices for their children's educational development.

1.1.5 Payment of rent

Many persons desire to live in their own houses, but the reality is that not everyone will be able to afford to do so, and some will have to settle for rented properties. Some persons intend to rent only for a period, but eventually they spend most of their lives, if not all, in a rented property.

Those who do not have their own houses may be required to pay rent. Some persons may be fortunate enough to live in their parents' or family's houses and not have to pay rent, since their family just wants someone to stay in the property.

Paying rent can be a challenging thing. Most times, persons have to pay their rent monthly, so they have to get a constant flow of income to pay their rent. Those who are working will have the opportunity to earn money regularly, which is expected to cover the cost of their rent.

1.1.6 Payment for security services

Within some communities, there may be burglaries. As a result, some residents will choose to incur costs to protect their assets. While guards are one option, some individuals may opt to use security cameras for their protection. Whichever option persons choose, they will have to incur some costs for security.

No one knows when a burglary will strike on their assets, so they should look for every opportunity to protect their property. The cost to replace many assets will constantly increase, so protection costs through a guard may be lower than replacement costs.

1.1.7 Repairs and maintenance of vehicle and property

Regular and timely maintenance of assets is important to keep them functioning properly. Some persons may establish schedules to repair particular assets. For example, vehicles that are used daily may have to be serviced monthly, especially if the vehicle has to travel long distances.

Some persons may choose to wash their house at least once a year or repaint it every three to five years. The constant maintenance of one's assets allows them to have competitive market values.

It can be costly to maintain some assets. Therefore, some persons will seek employment to earn enough money to repair and maintain their assets.

1.1.8 Increase in academics

Not everyone wants to maintain the same academics with which they left secondary school. Some persons might go on to college and complete additional studies. When persons want to further their learning and obtain certificates for academic and professional studies, they will have to spend time studying and writing examinations. This exercise will cost money as well as time. People must treat their costs for studies as investment costs, which can make their future great. Studying is often hard work, but it results in success that will outweigh the money and time spent studying.

In some homes, both the father and the mother may be studying. They plan to be an example to their children, as they know that studying will provide them with opportunities to earn more.

1.1.9 Acquisition of a vehicle

Some persons plan that their use of public transportation will only be temporary. Therefore, they have a timeline for when they will want to acquire their own vehicle.

Some persons work because it is their only way to earn enough to get a vehicle. If they were to depend on the small income they receive from family members, then they may not have enough money for a vehicle and will have to continue using public transportation.

For some persons, as they work, they will replace their vehicles from time to time. Those who are entitled to duty-free concessions may have a set time when they will replace their vehicles.

1.1.10 Acquisition of property

Not everyone may see acquiring a vehicle as a priority. However, many persons would like to have their own property, so they will earn money that will allow them to purchase property. To acquire property may require some sacrifices, but some persons are already prepared to make those sacrifices, as they know at the end of it, they will have their own property.

1.1.11 Savings and investments

Persons may challenge themselves not to be working for the rest of their lives. Therefore, as they earn, they may make some investments. Other persons may not want to take too many risks, so they may choose not to have investments, but instead to save any extra funds that they have earned.

Most times, investments made now will produce benefits for the future. Those who may have one property may choose to acquire more properties from their additional funds.

1.1.12 Financing their parents and other relatives

Some parents may not be able to work. Therefore, they expect that those family members that are working will assist them.

Some children are willing to contribute to their parents without needing to be asked. Children must not be burdened to finance their parents, but it should be a decision that each child will make.

Within families, there may be relatives who need financial support. Therefore, family members who can earn and support those relatives who need support may choose to seek employment so that they can assist their relatives. No one should feel comfortable financially when they have relatives who are struggling financially and may need some small one-off financial support.

1.1.13 Creating a pension for their future benefits

Most times, the government will pay a pension to those persons who have worked or reached the pensionable age. Therefore, if persons want to have a decent pension, then they may have to work and make pension contributions. It may appear burdensome to some persons that they have to pay regular pension contributions, but they are working towards giving themselves a great financial future after they reach the retirement age.

1.1.14 Payment of fire, medical, and life insurance

Insurance will not prevent certain events from occurring. However, if those events occur, then those who have insured their assets will get some compensation for any costs incurred. Sometimes, medical expenses can be very high. Therefore, many persons will work so that if they become ill, they can be covered by their medical insurance.

Those who have assets may have to take out life and fire insurance. This may encourage persons to work so that they have enough money to meet those financial needs.

1.1.15 Contributions to religious organizations and social groups

Those who belong to religious or social groups may be required to make regular financial contributions, even if the amounts are small. Persons who join clubs may have to pay club dues, and those who are part of religious organizations may be required to make contributions or donations.

Those who are employed will have money to contribute to their religious or social groups. The amounts and timing of the payments may vary, but each member will be expected to make contributions at least once per year.

2. Other benefits

A person may decide to work because they need money to take care of their financial needs. However, as they work, they may recognize that they will also receive other benefits. These benefits will not be the same amount as their wages and salaries. However, each financial benefit may add up to something important. Some of these benefits may even continue when an employee is on sick leave or has retired.

2.1 Career development and sponsorship

Employees may be sponsored by their employers to attend seminars. These training sessions are geared towards equipping employees to become effective and efficient for the organization. Most employers do not mind investing in employees who show promising signs that they will help the organization to be productive.

Some career development sessions can be for a few weeks, while other sessions can last for years. For example, employers may invest in some employees to complete a degree program or a master's degree. The full cost of this program will be paid by the employer, and the employee will have to be committed to serve a certain number of years with the organization.

Some persons join organizations at the entry level, but because of their performance, management may send them for career development. Once the training is completed, they may be promoted to senior positions, which means they will be entitled to a significant pension after they retire.

2.2 Medical benefits

Some organizations have established agreements with other organizations to provide medical services to their employees. The medical benefits will only be available to permanent employees, since casual and temporary employees will not have earned the right to receive this benefit. Most times, casual and temporary employees will have to prove that they are capable of being employed with the organization on a long-term basis.

Medical benefits offered by organizations may include:

- Optical care
- Dental service
- Pregnancy and childbirth

On many occasions, employers will pay part of the medical expenses, and employees will pay the other part. Employees are sometimes willing to pay their medical contributions because they know that the benefits that they receive will be greater than the amount of their contributions. Once the employee resigns or retires, then this benefit ceases.

2.3 Sales commissions

Sales commissions are performance-related pay. This employment benefit requires employees to deliver multiple products, sell a targeted number of products, produce a specific quantity of products, etc. Sales commissions may be based upon a percentage, which may vary depending upon the employee's level of achievement. For example, if an employee meets the sales target for the month, they may be entitled to 15% of the products sold for the month.

There are other situations where employees will be paid sales commission in a fixed amount, based upon various targets reached. For example, if a sales agent surpasses their target of $1,000,000, then they will be entitled to $10,000, or if an employee surpasses the target of $800,000, then they will be entitled to $5,000. When employees' sales commissions are aligned to targets, then employees will constantly work to meet or surpass those targets so that they can benefit from additional compensation.

2.4 Bonuses

In many organizations, bonuses may be another performance-related benefit. For this type of benefit, the employee has to complete some activities, and if the organization meets or surpasses its target, then employees may be entitled to bonuses. Some organizations will offer a year-end bonus to their employees, which may not be directly related to the performance of an individual.

Employees are often happy when they receive bonuses. These bonuses may be paid at the end of the organization's fiscal year, and some may be subject to different taxation rates.

2.5 Pensions

Pensions are a benefit that is subject to certain conditions. These conditions may include that employees must be permanent employees and have worked for a specific amount of time with the organization. For example, employees may have to work at least one year before joining the pension scheme. Those who join the pension scheme may benefit from the employer's contribution after they complete a specific number of years, for example, at least five continuous years. Employees' contributions to the pension scheme may be based upon a percentage or a fixed amount. For example, employees may have to pay 5% of their gross salary as their pension contribution. There are other organizations where employees have to pay a fixed amount, for example, $2,000 monthly for those whose monthly salary is above $15,000.

When an employee retires, they will receive regular payouts based upon the pension scheme. For example, retirees may be paid their pension every month. Some persons who are retired may spend most of their time relaxing and living on the regular pension payouts, since they do not have any major commitments and their children may all be living with their new families.

2.6 Long service awards

Employees who choose to remain with an organization in the good and not-so-good times may benefit from long service awards. These awards may be given in monetary form or something else that allows the employee to remember the years served at the organization.

The minimum years that an employee has to work for the organization to receive such an award may be ten years or longer. What is important is that employees will receive this benefit if they continue to work with the organization.

Management may be willing to provide these benefits to employees because they know that their employees have the option of changing organizations, but they choose to stay. Management may also consider that these long-serving employees have great institutional knowledge, which will help the organization in the future. When persons join organizations and then leave, it often disrupts the work program, as the learning curve may be very steep for new employees. The cost to train new employees will far outweigh the costs of the long service awards.

3. Friendship

Employees sometimes see their workplace as their second home, because they have the opportunity to establish friendships with many persons. Within some homes, there may only be a few family members, and the conversations may keep repeating the same information. However, when an employee chooses to establish friendships with other employees, they have many more things to discuss.

Some employees are excited to attend work regularly because they have many friends there. They may even see their workmates as a second family. Over time, workplace friends tend to look out for each other, as they want to protect their friends or help them to do the right things.

Figure 3. Types of stakeholders to establish friendships at the workplace

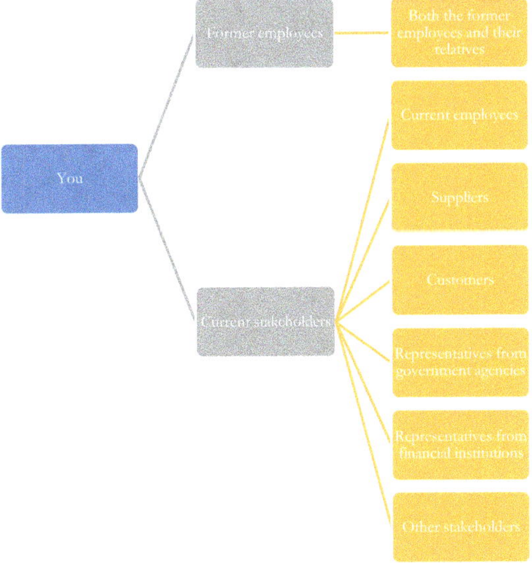

3.1 Former employees

When an employee has been working for an organization for some months or years, there may be other employees who reach the age of retirement, resign, or are let go by management. Therefore, these employees will no longer be employed by the organization, but that does not stop current employees from connecting with them. Some current employees have learned so much from those persons that even after their departure from the organization, they stay connected.

3.1.1 Both the former employees and their relatives

The friendship with a former employee has no set timeline, since it can continue until death. It can even grow to the point where current employees are communicating with former employees' companions, children, and other care providers. As persons retire or become aged, they may not be able to do many things independently for themselves, so they may need a care provider. If persons have the time, they may assist their relatives who are aged and unable to help themselves. Many children often help their aged parents in whatever way they can.

With good friendships between current and former employees, current employees may visit the homes of former employees to physically check on them. There are also times when current and former employees may meet at social events or in the markets.

Friendships with former employees may provide a rich source of information for current employees. Some former employees are willing to share their professional and personal experiences with current employees.

These friendships may even extend to the former employee's children and other family members. For example, if the child of a former employee is about to be married, then wedding invitations may be sent to selected current employees. When former employees are deceased, some current employees may be in contact with their relatives, and their relationship may even grow after the time of bereavement.

3.2 Current stakeholders

As a person works, they have many opportunities to establish friendships with current stakeholders. Each person will determine who they want to maintain a good working relationship with.

3.2.1 Current employees

Many persons choose to work because they need good friendships with their fellow employees. These employees may treat each other as important friends and will constantly do things to foster the growth of their friendship. Even if they have disagreements, they may try to mend their friendships as quickly as possible.

Friendships with other current employees can be very large in number. Some employees maintain a friendship with employees at all levels within the organization, as they know that everyone ought to be important to them. The significance and importance of conversations may vary across the levels of employees, but there is still the need to connect with as many current employees as possible.

Figure 4. Friendships with all levels of current employees

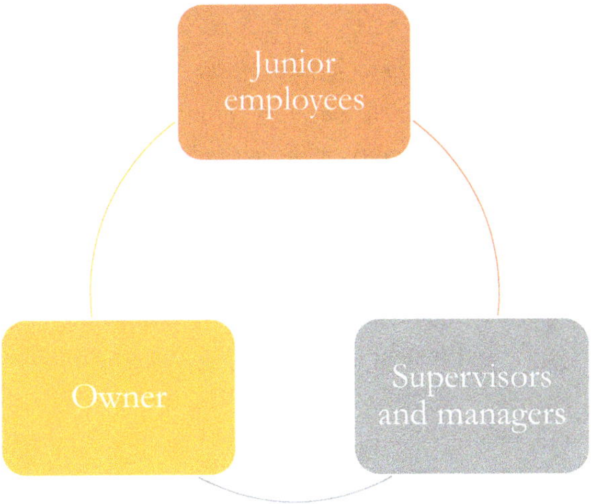

When the owner is directly involved in the organization, some employees may establish friendships with that person. In organizations where there is a partnership or corporation, some employees may have to interact with those owners, and friendships may be established. Some employees are mainly interested in establishing relationships with the owners, rather than the junior employees. They will establish relationships with supervisors, managers, and owners because they have their own agenda and may be looking for favors.

However, the nature of some employees' work will cause them to interact regularly with the supervisors, managers, and owners. For example, if senior employees have to physically approve certain documents, then junior employees may have to interact with them regularly, and their work friendship may grow.

3.2.2 Suppliers

Some employees enjoy working as it enables them to connect with other stakeholder groups, and one such group is suppliers. For example, some suppliers will have direct interaction with certain employees, as they have to collect items from or deliver products to the organization. Friendships between suppliers and employees may develop since the organization will have to pay the supplier for the products supplied. Whenever more products are needed, Purchase Orders (PO) will be prepared and dispatched to suppliers, and a representative of the organization will deliver the product.

3.2.3 Customers

The nature of some businesses may provide a direct connection between customers and employees. For example, sales representatives and cashiers will have to interact with many customers. When a customer frequently visits the organization, their friendships with particular employees will grow. Some employees will enjoy their interactions with customers since there are so many things that they can learn from the customers or share with them.

Being a front-line employee may create a direct connection with many customers. Some of these customers may take time to express their appreciation for the services the employees provide. There are times when employees may be having a challenging day, but their interactions with customers boost their confidence and give them hope. Caring customers often go beyond purchasing a product or collecting a service to find out how the employee is doing that day. Some caring customers may interact with a selected number of employees constantly, and if something is affecting them, those customers may notice and reach out to to them to provide support or comfort.

Many persons seek employment because when they are having a challenging day, even if it is the result of something personal that they are experiencing, they may have comfort at the end of the day after they have interacted with certain customers. Employees may experience that some customers are very good at motivating them and sharing quality information with them.

3.2.4 Representatives from government agencies

Not all employees may have to interact with representatives of government agencies. However, those who do have these interactions may enjoy their regular time of conversing.

Managers and supervisors may be invited to events organized by the government. At trade expos and other collaborative events between organizations and government agencies, friendships between representatives from government agencies and employees of the organization may strengthen, as they have to work together to showcase products or interact with those who need more information about the event.

3.2.5 Representatives from financial institutions

Those who are employed and have to interact with representatives from financial institutions may develop friendships as these interactions continue. Most times, these conversations are professional, but as their interaction grows, they may be able to have a fun moment during their conversation to talk about something that is not work-related. If both persons have to talk regularly with each other, then they may not even have to state their names on the telephone when they call each other because they are familiar with each other's voices, so the conversation will flow easily between them. Sometimes, the interaction between these employees may provide comfort if one of them is experiencing a difficult situation.

3.2.6 Other stakeholders

Most organizations have multiple stakeholders. From time to time, some of these other stakeholders will have to interact with employees of the organization. Some organizations have union representatives, so the trade union will constantly connect with the employees to know if they are fairly treated and identify what more the trade union can do to help the organization.

3.3 Why build friendships when you are employed?

Some employees are not interested in building friendships at work. They will go to work and try to keep to themselves. If they do not like interacting with many persons, they will often avoid getting to know more about them or trying to help them.

However, there are many reasons to build friendships in the workplace. For example, in times of sickness, there may be the need to talk with another workmate. Employees who are parents may have many things that they will confidentially share with each other. During their discussions, enough possible options may be offered that some challenges can be resolved.

For holidays, employees may agree to have their own social gatherings. These gatherings may allow them to get to know each other better and also equip them with some important life skills.

In times of sickness, some employees may be able to visit their workmates who are sick and offer them some comforting words. There are times when employees may also pray for those who are sick.

Those who are working have many opportunities to be in regular interactions with their workmates. When mothers give birth, they may be visited by workmates who may bring gifts or cards for them. When an employee is about to be married, they may receive some important advice from those who are already married, which may prove essential for their new journey into family life. Employees sometimes will give monetary donations to their workmates who are about to be married.

If an employee has completed some studies, then there may be a time of celebration at the workplace. Those employees who have studied know the challenges of working and studying. Sometimes, employees who are studying may have a companion and children. However, they may be studying because they want to improve their earnings and standard of living.

4. Relationships

Many persons have no intention of looking for a companion at the workplace, but there is a possibility that they may find one. There are so many strange and important things that happen as persons work. Many persons may remember that while they were doing their work, their conversations and interactions sparked interest in their workmates. Sometimes, from one conversation, many other things cause two persons to be connected, and then they proceed to begin a relationship that can lead to marriage.

Figure 5. Options for finding a companion at work

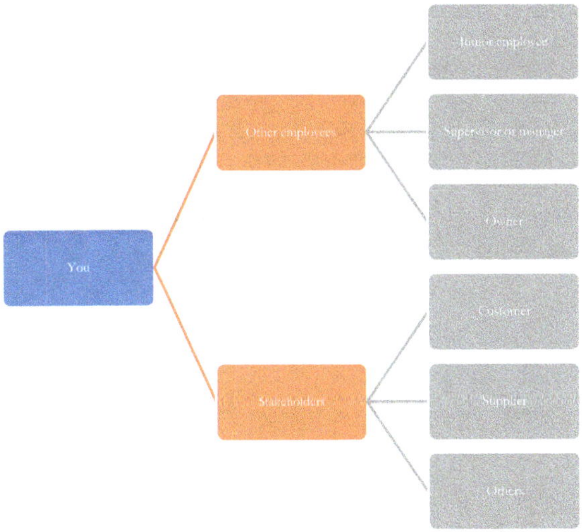

4.1 Other employees

Within every organization, there will be employees working at various levels. Most organizations will have a mixture of female and male employees. There are a few organizations that will only employ persons of one gender, but whenever there is a mixture of men and women, it creates an opportunity for persons to possibly find a companion.

4.1.1 Junior employees

Junior-level employees may have to work along with other employees at the same level. As they continue their daily activities, they may share some of their likes and dislikes. There may be opportunities for them to attend training courses together on behalf of the organization. Sometimes, these employees may use the same public transportation to travel to and from work.

Within some organizations, junior employees may visit the same lunch room, and that may provide an opportunity for them to share ideas. Sometimes, junior employees may attend the same gym as they work to keep themselves fit.

Junior employees who are sportsmen and sportswomen may attend the same event. They may be sponsored by their organization, so they may train together or have to compete against different teams.

Many of these workplace interactions among junior employees may create opportunities for courtship and companionship.

4.1.2 Supervisor or manager

Due to the nature of many employees' work, they will have to interact with supervisors and managers. While they are occupied completing the work for the organization, there may be occasions for them to discuss their personal development and preferences. From month to month or year to year, some work-related friendships may evolve into personal relationships.

The nature of some work may cause some employees to work closely with each other. For example, some junior employees may have to take physical documents to their supervisor or manager for approval. As they see each other regularly and talk, they may develop a personal interest in each other and begin a relationship.

4.1.3 Owner

Sometimes, there may be an employee who has a personal interest in the owner. Those who have such a personal interest may look for work opportunities to make their interest known. On the other hand, some owners are also interested in having a relationship with an employee.

When many persons first join an organization, they may not be interested in having a relationship with a workmate, but because they spend so many hours at work that it becomes their second home, they may become personally connected. For example, organizations may have social events that employees are expected to attend, which may require them to wear something other than their working attire. On some of these occasions, employees may have opportunities to participate in sports or dancing. With all of these work-related activities, some employees may soon develop a personal interest in a workmate.

4.2 Stakeholders

While some organizations may have few stakeholders, others have many. Most stakeholders will visit the organization to conduct their business, but sometimes, the professional way employees treat the stakeholders can cause them to return a kind gesture to the employees, and that may spark some interest between them.

4.2.1 Customer

Customers may have to visit the organization regularly for business transactions. In other cases, employees may have to frequently visit or call certain customers. As employees and customers interact frequently, they may develop an interest in each other and start a relationship.

4.2.2 Supplier

Suppliers may also have to interact with employees, similar to customers. These interactions may be professional at the beginning, but over time, the supplier and an employee may develop a relationship with one another.

4.2.3 Others

Employees may have to interact with government agencies, medical institutions, or insurance companies, and this interaction may create avenues for persons to show some personal interest in each other.

4.3 Why employees may choose a workmate as their companion

Some employees will not date someone who works at the same organization. They may have their own reasons for this, but love has a way of connecting people regardless of their status and education, since love has no borders. Therefore, while many employees may never think about getting into a relationship with a fellow employee, their work may create avenues for them to communicate with each other. Sometimes, one interaction may lead to months of regular communication and then a relationship.

Figure 6. Why employees may choose a workmate as their companion

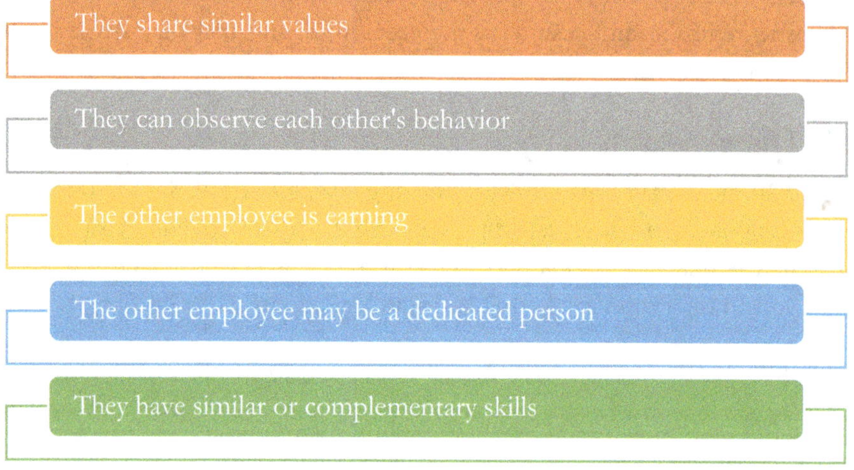

4.3.1 They share similar values

Some persons will choose their companion because of what the person earns, while others need someone who knows their value and has similar values. Money is not the only thing that contributes to the success of any relationship, since many persons with much money find it difficult to maintain their relationships.

The values that some persons stand for may be their winning point that has caught the attention of their future companion. For example, some employees are mannerly, always willing to go the extra mile to help others, always keeping the work area tidy, etc. These little things that some employees do while working may prompt someone to take interest in them. There are some employees whose attire and hairstyle always look neat, and that may cause other employees to be more interested in them.

4.3.2 They can observe each other's behavior

Some persons are in long-distance relationships, where each person lives in a different community or country. These relationships require each partner to have great trust in the other, and it is expected that both persons will be honest, even when no one is seeing them.

However, when employees choose someone who works with the same organization, they will be better able to observe each other. They may be able to eat and travel together every day. These few daily interactions among employees can be the starting point of a relationship.

Too many persons are excited to rush into a relationship without observing their companion. Sometimes, when they are fully committed to the relationship, then they see some reactions that were always present, but which they had not noticed. While two individuals of opposite genders may have similar values, there may be some things that the other person does not find acceptable. Therefore, each employee must take some time to observe the other, and when they are reasonably satisfied, then they can proceed with the relationship.

4.3.3 The other employee is earning

With the need to find money to pay for so many expenses, it can become difficult for only one family member to be earning. Within some homes, both parents may be working, yet they find it difficult to adequately address all of the family's expenditures.

When persons want to choose a companion, they often want to know that they have found someone who can add financial resources to the relationship. There are a few persons who may ask their companion to stop working after they marry. However, for most other relationships, both persons may work to take care of the family's needs.

4.3.4 The other employee may be a dedicated person

If a person is not dedicated to their work, then they may not be dedicated to their relationship with their companion either. When persons are looking for a long-term relationship, they typically want to know that the person they choose will be there for them and will support the family financially.

Persons who like to absent themselves from work for no justifiable reason may want to take a similar approach to their relationship. The confidence and growth in many relationships are dependent upon the commitment that each person shows toward their partner.

4.3.5 They have similar or complementary skills

At some workplaces, multiple employees may have the same skills. Because of their commonality, they may find that their skills complement each other, so if they join in a relationship, then they will make a great combination.

Not everyone may choose to stay with their employer until they retire. There are some employees who would like to establish their own businesses. Therefore, they will need someone who has complementary skills to work with them. If two employees form a relationship and seriously consider establishing their own business, then they may resign from the organization to focus on their business.

5. Getting away from stress and family challenges

Even if someone's needs are well met in a home, they may still have to endure much stress and family challenges. They believe that if they have the opportunity to work, then they will ease themselves of some of those challenges.

5.1 Stress with children

Many persons need children, but not everyone will have them. Parents may speak of the joy that their children bring to their hearts. However, some persons will prefer to work so that they are away from the challenges that their children produce.

Parents can spend time training children, but it does not guarantee that their children will always display good attributes. The training of children must not be left to one parent; rather, both parents should be actively involved in guiding the future of their children. Parents should also avoid having disagreements in front of their children.

When children do the wrong things, both parents must let them know that their behavior in this particular situation is not acceptable. If only one parent is involved in disciplining the children, then it may appear to be too much for that parent to manage sometimes.

When some children become young adults, they may cause their parents many problems. Despite the parents taking time to properly raise their children, some of them can follow friends who will lead them in the wrong direction. These young adults' behavior may be unacceptable to their parents, so some parents will choose to work so that they can avoid being at home every day to deal with such behaviors.

5.2 Stress with a companion

When persons are coming together in a relationship, their behaviors may be well accepted. However, as the relationship grows older, one partner may display some behaviors that are not expected from them as a family person. For example, one partner may be using alcohol or an illegal substance. This may be annoying to their partner, and this behavior may force their partner to seek employment as a form of comfort.

Some partners will argue about almost anything, which may be stressful for the other partner. No relationship is perfect, but not many persons can endure being in the same house and having to deal with family situations when there seems to be no end to the problems.

5.3 Stress with other family members

Persons who are living in an extended-family household may have problems with other family members. For example, if the extended family includes a mother-in-law, father-in-law, nephews, and nieces, then this may place strain on persons who want to manage their family in a particular way.

Due to some persons' financial situations, they may not be able to rent or purchase their own house. Therefore, they may eventually spend some time living with their in-laws, hoping that life will become better for them. However, if there are many family conflicts, then some persons may choose work, which will give them some time away from the stresses at home.

The workplace can become a haven for persons who are encountering many problems at home. The daily problems at home may be overwhelming for some persons, and they may perceive that being employed is the best solution to these challenges.

5.4 Regular conversation

For some persons, when they are at home, they are alone. While some persons wish that they could stay at home and still have enough money to take care of their needs, others want to work because they are tired of being at home.

For example, if one parent had to stay home to attend to their toddlers, that need will no longer exist when the children become adults. When those children are working, the house can become a lonely place for the parent who once stayed home to look after them, as it can be feel lonely to be in the house for most of the day without anyone to talk with. This loneliness may be strange to them, since a few months or years ago, there were children in the house to keep them company, but the house is now empty since those children are working or have their own families. Therefore, the stay-at-home parent will now seek employment so that they can use that extra time that they have.

Some parents go through a phase where they have much joy when their children are young, but when those children become older and establish new friends, they will spend less time communicating with their parents. Those parents who are alone at home may now join the workforce as they need persons to talk to. They want to know that someone is listening to them and that they will get some feedback.

Parents who seek employment may choose between part-time and full-time work, based upon their family commitment. For example, the stay-at-home parent may have children who are in the nursery stage of learning and may only be required to spend the first half of the day at school and then return home to their parents. When children move into primary school, they will spend longer periods at school but will be home in the mid-afternoon. Therefore, based upon this timing, some parents will seek part-time employment to keep themselves occupied for that short duration.

When persons are employed, they may have opportunities to interact with other employees, customers, and suppliers. Those who use public transportation may also have the opportunity to converse with other travelers.

Regular conversations may ease someone's stress. In some relationships, one partner may be at home to attend to the children, while the other is working many miles away, or even in another country. Therefore, the partners have less face-to-face contact. In such a case, spending time working may be important, as they get to share ideas and learn from others.

6. Exercise

Among those who engage in regular exercise, many are disciplined enough to start their training and continue until they accomplish their target, but others may need more motivation.

6.1 Persons should consider exercising

Many persons are procrastinating about exercising. However, they should consider exercising today instead of leaving it for many more years. Persons can become sick because they refuse to take care of their health. Many persons will spend money to wear clothes that make them look great, but they spend less money to take care of their health. Persons may spend time watching the news, movies, and sports, but not make a sacrifice to exercise.

Figure 7. Why should persons exercise?

6.1.1 Reduce excess weight

Persons who are at home may find themselves consuming food regularly, as long as they can afford to purchase the groceries they need. At home, it can be easy to walk to the fridge or pot and take something to eat at any time. However, if that same person is working, they do not have the option to eat and drink constantly, since the work will keep them occupied.

Most persons are conscious of their weight. If they have gained weight, then they need to exercise. The types and frequency of exercise may vary for each individual, but they must manage their weight, especially if they are overweight. Many times, it is easy to increase one's weight, but it takes much discipline to reduce that excess weight.

6.1.2 Keep yourself fit

Besides exercising to lose weight, some persons exercise to keep themselves in shape, which can be a good habit to develop. Sometimes, the types of exercise to keep a person fit may not be rigorous as exercising to reduce excess weight. For example, persons may engage in activities within their yard or garden to keep fit. They may not want to go to the gym, but as they take care of the plants, remove leaves from under the trees, or wash their vehicle, they are exercising.

Other persons will deliberately enroll at a gym to keep themselves fit. They will go through routine exercise so that certain parts of their body will have a specific size and shape.

6.1.3 Keep yourself healthy

Exercising contributes to keeping a person healthy. Many persons may be sitting down or spending too much time in bed, which can cause them to develop health issues. Therefore, as persons choose to exercise, they can reduce their medical bills and keep themselves healthy.

Those who are constantly keeping themselves active may not have much to do to keep themselves healthy. However, those who have not exercised for a long time may need to start exercising.

If a person is injured and has to receive medical assistance, the doctor will advise them to exercise as part of their healing. As they continue to do their exercises, very soon they may be able to benefit from the full use of that part of their body once again. Both medication and exercising are good to keep persons healthy, so do not neglect one for the other.

6.1.4 Improve your memory capacity

Not everyone may be affected by problems with remembering things. However, as a personal exercise, they may give themselves opportunities to improve or strengthen their ability to think quickly.

There are persons who are retired and are exercising. If they are not walking, they may be riding or swimming. Some of them may play Scrabble or crossword puzzles as well, to keep both their brain and their body functioning properly.

6.1.5 Enhance your quality of sleep

Sleeping can be difficult for some persons. However, exercise may allow them to have an enjoyable rest. Some persons will choose to exercise in the afternoon and evening. After they finish exercising, then they may eat a light snack, have a bath, and go to bed. They have prepared themselves to have a comfortable rest because they have burned some energy before going to bed.

6.1.6 Reduce fatigue and manage mental health

Mental health remains a big challenge for both young and old persons. However, to help balance their mental health, they can choose to exercise. Their choice of exercise may not be anything strenuous or frequent, but even light exercise can reduce signs of fatigue.

Many persons easily become stressed by worrying about problems. They often respond to small problems in unusual ways. However, as they exercise, they may find that their responses to the same problems will be different. For example, parents can become very stressed, especially when they have to deal with many challenges. Some single parents may find it especially difficult to cope with some problems, since they may not have any other adult to share their concerns with. However, if they choose to exercise, they may provide themselves with opportunities to remain calm over the same problems.

6.2 Reasons why a person may quit exercising

Sadly, while exercising is good for everyone, some persons quit exercising. Humans sometimes know what is good for them, yet they choose to do different things and only cause themselves much pain for the future. It is important to examine why some persons may quit exercising.

Figure 8. Why persons quit exercising

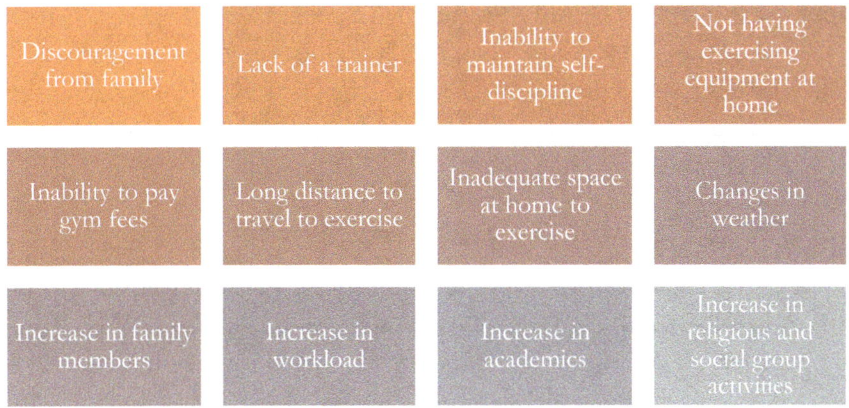

6.2.1 Discouragement from family

Many persons will expect family members to be there to support them, but that is not always true. The words said by family members can be disturbing to some persons and cause them to quit exercising. Strangers may say bad things to others, but when a family member says a similar thing, it may hurt more than what a stranger will say.

There are some persons who know that a member of their family is trying very hard to reduce excess weight, but it may take them some time to do so, and instead of encouraging them to continue, they will use insulting words. This will cause their family member to quit exercising, since they have lost confidence in themselves.

6.2.2 Lack of a trainer

Not everyone is disciplined enough to exercise alone. Some persons may join a gym and have an instructor to work with. However, if they are unable to have the support of a gym instructor, then they will not continue exercising. There are times when a gym instructor will choose not to continue guiding trainees. They may resign from the gym, thus leaving many trainees without instructors.

6.2.3 Inability to maintain self-discipline

Those who want to exercise must be aware that they have to be self-disciplined. There are days when they may not feel like exercising, but they have to push themselves beyond those feelings and exercise. Sometimes, friends and family members may discourage those who are exercising, but if they want to remain healthy, then they have to exercise.

In the homes of some persons, they have their own gym equipment, but they lack the self-discipline to exercise. They may sleep longer than they should or eat more than they should, but they refuse to give much attention to exercising on a routine basis.

6.2.4 Not having exercising equipment at home

Persons may enroll at a gym and enjoy their regular exercises. However, the time allocated to them may not be sufficient, or they may not be able to spend much time at the gym. If they had gym equipment at home, they would continue to exercise.

Persons may not be able to afford gym equipment, so they do not have it at home. Other persons may not have space at home for their own gym equipment, so that may restrict them from exercising.

6.2.5 Inability to pay gym fees

For many gyms, the fees may be reasonable enough to attract many persons. However, some persons are still struggling to meet their basic financial needs. If persons lose their jobs or their expenses increase, then they may not have enough money to pay gym fees. Even if the gym fees are low, not everyone is in a position to pay, as they may have several competing expenses to address regularly.

6.2.6 Long distance to travel to exercise

If persons have to travel a long distance to exercise, they may start out enjoying that travel. However, they may become distracted as they begin to consider the same distance to be too long.

If a person does not have access to their own transportation, they may feel that the distance is too long to travel when they have to use public transportation. Some persons have friends who can transport them to the gym for regular exercise. However, if those friends are unable to transport them in the future, then they may quit, since the distance may be too long for them to travel using public transportation.

6.2.7 Inadequate space at home to exercise

When persons' families are expanding, they may soon run out of space to do many of the things they want to do. For example, when a couple has just started their relationship, it may be just the two of them alone, with room in the house to set up gym equipment for those who want to exercise. However, as the couple has children, the room that once contained the gym equipment may be converted for another function. Once that gym equipment is no longer accessible to the adults in the home, they may quit exercising.

6.2.8 Changes in weather

Some persons enjoy exercising in the open space, where they have access to the natural environment. They may walk a long distance in a park or in their communities, as long as the weather is conducive. However, if there is a major shift in the weather, they may postpone exercising for a few days, hoping that the weather will improve. If the weather does not improve soon, they may quit exercising instead of looking for other options to continue exercising until the weather improves.

6.2.9 Increase in family members

Many fathers and mothers are guilty of not exercising as much as they once did. Their reason for reducing or quitting exercise is that the numbers of their family has increased. Indeed, with the addition of more children, parents will have to spend much of their time attending to their children. The demands of caring for children can be very challenging, as each child will have their own needs and expectations that their parents will have enough time to spend with them.

When parents have to give more time to their children, they may reduce or quit their exercise routine. Many parents plan to put a temporary pause on exercising, but may not return to their exercise routine because of their family commitments.

6.2.10 Increase in workload

Many persons are often looking for an increase in compensation, but a pay raise often comes with an increase in workload. Those who have increased their skills and academics may be promoted. However, once they are promoted, they have more work to manage.

With an increase in workload, persons may spend long hours at their workplace. When they return home, they are tired and may just want to eat and then rest immediately.

Some persons want to accomplish certain things before they reach retirement age. Therefore, they may work longer hours to increase their earnings. Those who are living in rented houses may want to construct their own houses, so they may work two jobs to earn enough money.

6.2.11 Increase in academics

Not everyone is comfortable with their current level of academics. Therefore, they may choose to enroll in additional courses, which means they will have to spend more time studying. As more time is allocated towards studying, less time is spent on exercising.

6.2.12 Increase in religious and social group activities

Persons may begin dedicating more time to religious or social activities. As they spend more time on these activities, they may quit exercising. For example, if a person takes up administrative functions in clubs, then they may be occupied with planning, reading minutes, typing minutes, listening to members' concerns, etc. These activities, while small, can take away the little time that a person had set aside for exercising.

6.3 Basic work-related activities that aid in exercising

Some persons seek employment because they know that they will have many opportunities to exercise. Even those who sit behind a desk still have some basic things that they can do for exercise.

Figure 9. Basic work-related activities that contribute to exercising

Preparing to attend work

Walking at the workplace

Walking to the transportation point

6.3.1 Preparing to attend work

If a person is employed, there are certain things they have to do before going to work each day. Even those who have their own business and work for themselves may have to do some of these activities, which will contribute to their daily exercise.

As simple as it may be, persons will have to wake up at a certain time and then go to the bathroom. Just going to the bathroom to have a shower will demand some movement. Some persons will prepare their own meals in the kitchen. As they walk from the fridge to the sink, to the stove, to the cupboard, they are exercising. These trips may be numerous for some persons, so they may do much exercising before they leave their homes to attend work.

6.3.2 Walking at the workplace

Not everyone is privileged enough to sit behind a desk at work. Many other employees will be involved in walking to different parts of the office, even if it means carrying one document from one staff member to another.

For lunch breaks, some employees may have to walk to the cafeteria, and this will cause them to burn some energy. Those who have to attend regular meetings may have to walk to and from the location where the meeting is held.

Those who work in the field, factory, or their clients' work site may have much exercising to do regularly.

6.3.3 Walking to the transportation point

Those who use public transportation may have to walk from their homes to the closest stop or station. For some persons, they may have to walk long distances, as public transportation does not pass close to their dwellings.

Even when persons park their vehicles within the organizations' compound, they will have to walk to the parking lot after they finish working or when they arrive at work in the mornings.

6.4 Avoiding weight gain while employed

All employees must be aware that it is very easy to gain weight from the food they eat at work. Therefore, they must be deliberate to manage their weight while they work, since it may take them much effort to get rid of excess weight.

Figure 10. How to avoid weight gain while working with an organization

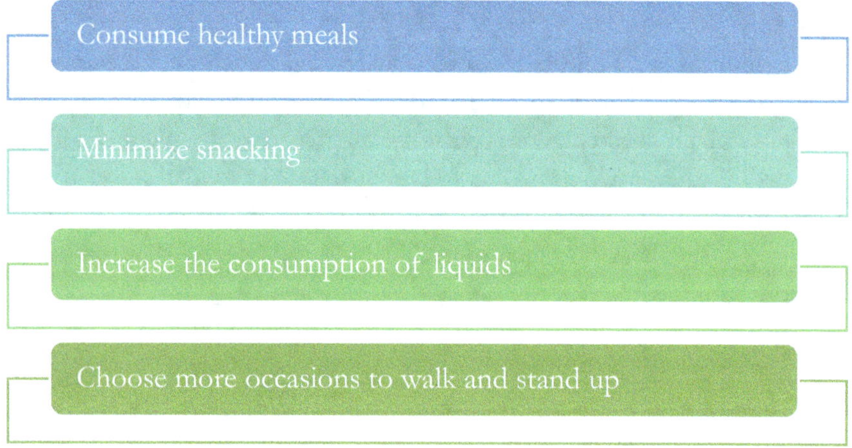

6.4.1 Consume healthy meals

Some persons consume many things that are not healthy for them. For example, a workmate may take some meals for other employees, and those meals may have a lot of carbohydrates or fat.

Persons who want to be health-conscious must be willing to say no to certain meals. Those meals may look tempting, but saying no may enable a person to live a long and healthy life. Persons who want to remain healthy may have charts and other documents to guide them concerning the major food groups. They may also have some examples of the different types of foods that can contribute to a healthy diet.

Table 1. There are five main groups of nutrients

Main groups of nutrients	Explanation	Sources of the nutrients
Protein	The primary function of protein is to provide body-building or growth materials, so every cell in the body contains proteins.	Meat, fish, cheese, eggs, wheat, rice, oats, beans
Fat (and oil)	Provides a convenient and concentrated source of energy, supplying more energy than the same weight of carbohydrate or protein.	Meat, butter, margarine, fish, nuts, fruits
Carbohydrate	Carbohydrates are the most important source of energy for the body. Almost all the cells of the body use glucose to distribute energy. Carbohydrate acts as a "protein sparer" so that protein can be used for its primary functions rather than as a source of energy.	Sugar, honey, molasses, jam, jelly, yam, sweet potato, breadfruit, rice, barley, corn

Vitamins	Vitamins are a group of chemical substances, most of which were identified during the 20th century as vital to the body. The body requires only small amounts of each vitamin. Vitamins can be classified according to the substances in which they dissolve.	Milk, cheese, eggs, carrot, spinach, watercress, cabbage, tomato, pumpkin, Callao, cod liver oil
Minerals	Bodybuilding. Control of bodily processes. Essential parts of body fluid. Some mineral elements are required in relatively large amounts.	Milk, cheese, broccoli, bok choy, legumes, bread

(Extract from Tull & Coward, 2009)

The health information in the table above must not only be read but be applied daily. Too many persons are spending their money to rectify health problems that they brought on themselves by consuming foods that did not contribute to a balanced diet.

6.4.2 Minimize snacking

Some persons will take their lunch to work, and they will also bring snacks. This may be good for some persons. However, the snacks that some persons take with them to work are just as big as their lunch, so they will be adding extra weight to themselves.

It is okay to say no to snacking, especially if you have already had breakfast. Snacking is not bad, but if it is not managed, then it will be harmful to anyone. Some persons will take fruit as their snacks. With this approach, they are ensuring that they get their vitamins from the fruit.

6.4.3 Increase the consumption of liquids

Persons must be deliberate to increase their consumption of liquids such as water and fruit juices. By drinking more liquids, there may be less space to overeat.

When persons are drinking liquids, they must check the nutritional contents. They must avoid too much sweetness in whatever beverages they will be consuming.

6.4.4 Choose more occasions to walk and stand up

When a person is at work, they must look for occasions where they can walk or stand. The work that some persons do may require them to sit most of the time. However, they must consider their health and take walks now and again. Getting up and walking for one to five minutes cannot prevent them from being productive every day. If the work is so demanding, then they can take their lunch breaks to get up and walk so that they get to exercise.

Always be willing to invest in your health, since many persons will not do it for you. Be deliberate to stay healthy and include exercise as part of your regular work life.

7. Finding your talent

Every individual has talent, but many persons may not know what their talent is. It may take persons many years to find their talent. Everyone should strive to know his or her talent at the earliest opportunity.

7.1 Activities that cause persons to find their talents

According to Fowler (1964), "talent" refers to a special aptitude, faculty, or gift. It is in this same context that the word "talent" will be discussed throughout this section of the literature.

Figure 12. Circumstances that result in a person finding their talent

Religious activities

Parents' involvement

Interactions with educators

Feedback from friends and enemies

Social, cultural, and sports activities

Employment opportunities

Challenges of life

7.1.1 Religious activities

When persons are involved in religious activities, they may recognize that they are doing something very easy that many persons may not be able to do.

Some persons may identify that the Creator has gifted them with special skills, or they may find their talent through the Creator. For example, some persons who are involved in religious activities may recognize that they like public speaking and that many persons enjoy listening to them. Other persons may engage in singing religious songs, and many persons are always excited to hear them sing.

It is through religious activities that some persons' talents are discovered and developed. Therefore, they will continue to engage in religious activities as they develop their talents and the lives of many persons are positively impacted.

7.1.2 Parents' involvement

Parental involvement might create a blossoming opportunity for children to identify their talents. Because parents spend most of the time with their children when they are younger, they have enough time and opportunities to see their children's talents grow.

Parents who recognize their children's talents may make investments for their children to improve on their talent. Sometimes, the investments parents make will give their children the confidence to become the best in their area of specialty.

Many children will listen to the advice of their parents. So, as parents constantly tell their children that they are talented in a particular area, those children will continue to ask their parents to evaluate their performance. Most parents will give their children honest feedback. If there is a need to correct their children, then parents will do so, but they will also provide comfort and support for their children to improve their talents.

7.1.3 Interactions with educators

At learning institutions, students will have regular interactions with their educators. As students become involved in their schoolwork or activities organized by the school, the educators may be able to identify their students' talents.

When educators inform students of their talents, it may confirm what those students already perceive, or it may be the first time a student recognizes that they have talent in that area. For example, when schools have debates, educators may identify that certain students can become lawyers, politicians, religious leaders, etc. While some students may not give much attention to the views shared by their educators, their parents and other persons may share the same views.

Many students spend considerable time at learning institutions; therefore, the educators have enough time to assess them. Some educators are also supportive in helping students develop their talents.

7.1.4 Feedback from friends and enemies

Many persons hate their enemies. However, if they were to listen to their enemies carefully, they may recognize that their enemies have helped them to identify their talents. Sometimes, enemies push persons into their talents, or persons may become enemies with others because of their talents. For example, if two persons are athletes, the one with superior talent may be hated by the other.

Friends can be another source of helping persons to identify their talents. Persons are often happy with the direction in which their friend is going and will do many things to help them to become better.

If persons spend much time with their friends, their friends may observe their talents and bring those talents to their attention. Some persons may be in denial, but later as they consider what their friends said to them, they may acknowledge that they have talent in that area. For example, if friends regularly organize social gatherings, one friend may often take the opportunity to prepare the meals. When the other friends taste the meal, they are aware that their friend has a talent for cooking and may want to establish a food shop or restaurant.

7.1.5 Social, cultural, and sports activities

Not everyone may have a desire to spend time in the house or the office. Some persons like to be involved in activities that occur away from the home or workplace.

On weekends and holidays, there may be cultural events that some persons will participate in, such as dancing and singing competitions. Karaoke is a way in which many persons may test their singing abilities. Sometimes, listeners may recognize the talent in someone who participates in karaoke singing.

At weddings and funerals, persons may be asked to be involved in different parts of the program. As they participate, many persons may enjoy their participation and engage them to do similar jobs.

Involvement in sports may allow many persons to find their talents. Not everyone will be a great sportsman or sportswoman, but some persons are so talented that their performances are outstanding compared to the other participants.

7.1.6 Employment opportunities

While some persons do not see any benefits in being employed, other persons are happy that they are employed. Through their employment, they have recognized and developed their talents. Today, some of those employees who have found their talents have gone on to occupy senior positions in the organization or now work for other employers.

There are many challenges in workplaces, but not everyone has the ability to fix them. Those who are able to fix challenges may be recognized and rewarded because of their talents. Therefore, employees must not be afraid of workplace challenges, since it may give them the opportunities to find their talents and resolve problems.

7.1.7 Challenges of life

Life is not perfect and never will be, so those who are looking for a perfect life must forget about it. There will be many challenges in life, and persons will do their best to fix them. However, that does not stop other challenges from surfacing.

In the case of drought, famine, flooding, and many other disasters, some persons may lose some of their assets or even their lives. However, other persons will find their talents, and their talents may fix the problems in their country and many others.

Those who always run from challenges may run straight into the arms of defeat, since some challenges are there to help some persons identify their talents. Therefore, see challenges as opportunities to blossom.

8. Developing your skills

At home, persons have the opportunity to increase their academics. They may also have more time to become a good sportsman or sportswoman. However, the working environment also provides them with many opportunities to make themselves great.

Working with an organization or a person can be challenging, but it also provides opportunities to grow. This growth may not happen overnight but over multiple years. When some persons first start working, their personal life is nothing much to be spoken about. However, as they work and take time to develop themselves, they become individuals that many persons would like to associate with. Some employers will be involved in recruiting talented employees because they know that those employees will make a great impact on the organization.

What persons must remember is that if they develop themselves, they may earn more and not have to work as hard as they currently do, since they will be working smarter. Therefore, they have the opportunity to start developing themselves now and enjoy the benefits that will be afforded to them as they continue to work for their employer.

8.1 Public speaking

Many employees can join clubs where they can learn to be more effective and efficient as they speak to the public. Some organizations will sponsor employees to develop their public speaking skills.

The nature of some people's jobs demands that they interact regularly with the public. As they regularly interact with many persons, they overcome their fear of talking to people and are willing to speak to large gatherings.

Figure 11. Employees' opportunities to develop their public speaking skills

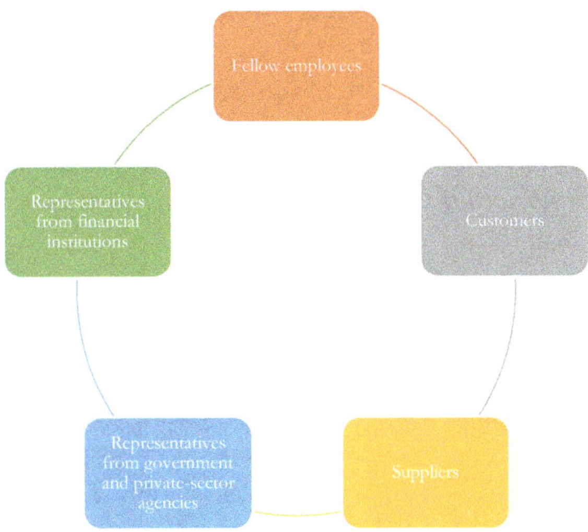

8.1.1 Fellow employees

As persons work, they have to interact with other employees. These regular interactions can cause them to become confident and able to speak to audiences within their communities and the nation.

Because of the good quality of their work, some junior employees may be promoted. When they are promoted, they will have meetings with their subordinates in which they will have to discuss matters and listen to the concerns of other employees.

Managers also develop their ability to communicate with the employees whom they lead. As managers and supervisors have regular meetings, they will learn how to become more effective in their communication with fellow employees.

8.1.2 Customers

Many organizations will have customers. On many occasions, customers will have to interact with junior employees or supervisors before they are allowed to communicate with the managers. With frequent interaction with customers, employees may become better at speaking to the public and sharing information.

8.1.3 Suppliers

Suppliers will often interact with employees. These interactions may be more frequent with junior employees than with senior employees. Some suppliers enjoy talking with junior employees because they get many of their concerns answered and junior employees may spend more time listening to them, whereas managers are often too busy.

8.1.4 Representatives from government and private-sector agencies

Employees may have to interact with representatives from government and private-sector agencies, perhaps frequently. Sometimes, government officials need specific information from an organization and may be directed to speak to specific employees.

There are times when government or private-sector representatives will visit some organizations to present some information. In that case, management may assign one of its employees to introduce the government representative at the meeting. This can be the start of many in-house training sessions for employees to practice their public speaking skills.

8.1.5 Representatives from financial institutions

Talking with persons from financial institutions on behalf of the organization may be another great opportunity to speak to external persons. Even if these conversations are not frequent, they may aid in the development of someone who can become a great public speaker.

8.2 Computer skills

Not everyone will have to use the computer at their workplace. While many persons purchase a computer for their personal use, they may not use many of its features. Persons may attend classes that taught them to use a computer, but they might not use those skills again after graduation.

However, employees who use computers at work will have opportunities to develop their skills. Some persons join organizations without any computer skills, but today, they are experts.

Persons may be skilled in using cellular phones, but using computers will require some different skills. Those skills can be learned and developed, but persons must be willing to practice as often as possible. The workplace provides constant opportunities for persons to grow in their computer skills.

8.3 Interaction and communication skills

When persons are living by themselves or with family members, they may not be too interested in communicating with others. Some persons prefer to isolate themselves. However, if those individuals are employed, they will have to interact with others. It is through these regular interactions that some employees can become bold or assertive.

Some persons are often bullied within their families, and they will take a quiet posture. However, as they work, they understand that they may have to state their views, even if others do not initially agree with them.

Communication requires the involvement of more than one person. Therefore, those who are working will have the opportunity to communicate. Persons must remember that communication does not mean that they have to do most of the talking. Those who are working may learn to be better listeners and only speak when it is necessary.

Non-verbal communication is another thing that employees will have to learn. Supervisors and managers may not always verbally state everything, perhaps using non-verbal communication to convey their messages instead. Below are some examples of non-verbal communication that can be used at the workplace or when persons are with their friends and relatives.

Table 2. Examples of non-verbal communication

Types of non-verbal communication	Examples
Facial expression	A smile, a frown
Gestures	Movement of hands and body to help to explain or emphasize our verbal message
Body posture	How we stand or sit
Orientation	Whether we face the other person or turn away
Eye contact	Whether we look at the other person or not, and the length of time that we look at the other person
Body contact	A pat on the back, an arm around the shoulder
Proximity	The distance we stand or sit from the person
Head nods	To indicate agreement or disagreement or to encourage the other to go on speaking
Appearance	Physical grooming and choice of clothes

Non-verbal aspects of speech	Variations of pitch, stress and timing; voice quality and tone of voice (these are sometimes called "para-language")
Non-verbal aspects of writing	Handwriting, layout, organization, neatness and visual appearance generally

(Extract from Stanton, 2009, p. 3)

When many persons are at home, they may not have to concentrate on their appearance. However, at work, they have to meet specific standards. For example, male employees may have to keep their hair low and to regularly trim their facial hair. Female employees may have to follow the organization's dress code, as uniforms may be provided.

Parents may experience challenges with their young adult children as it relates to their physical appearance. However, when those young adults have to work, they will comply with the standard way of dressing.

Some persons may not recognize that their body posture says something about them. However, when persons are employed, they know that they must demonstrate a certain body posture. For example, persons must not sit and slouch their shoulders, and they ought to sit erect in the office chair.

Before some persons were employed, they always appeared to have a serious face. However, as they have to interact with customers, they come to understand that smiling is important, and so they must have a pleasant face. This must not stop them from being serious when it is called for. Employees who are working for the military and paramilitary organizations may have to be serious on most occasions while on work-related duties. However, in many jobs, a smile can enhance communication between employees and those with whom they have to interact.

9. Regular motivation

Some persons may seek employment because they are demotivated and want to be away from any environment that makes them depressed. In some homes, persons may not feel the joy they expect to experience. Their community may be another place that they want to stay far away from. There is much violence in some communities, and that can cause some persons to feel uncomfortable living there.

9.1 To be motivated

When some persons attend work, they do so with the intention that someone will motivate them. They may not need daily motivation from others, but now and again, they need to find someone who will stir their passion to do good things. Many persons want to feel loved and cared for.

Some persons feel that no one cares for them or loves them. Some children are delighted when they reach the age to be employed, since they can provide for themselves and choose somewhere to spend most of their days, without anyone doing anything to discourage them.

The workplace can be good therapy for some persons who are demotivated. When they attend work, they may be greeted by the smiles of fellow employees who cheer them to do their best every single day. A few kind things may be enough to motivate employees who are demotivated. Sometimes a simple smile or pat on the back may make a great difference. When employees are going through financial difficulty, they may need many things to motivate them.

Leaders must be careful how they treat employees, since their words and actions may make some employees demotivated. On the other hand, some leaders will observe their employees and give compliments to those who appear to be demotivated.

9.2 To motivate others

Not everyone may be on the receiving end of needing to be motivated. Other persons will enjoy their time of working, as they are there to motivate others. They are there to lift the confidence of their fellow employees.

When an employee has a death in their family, they may need others to motivate them, and some employees are good at putting their workmates' minds at ease during a difficult situation. When an employee is sick, they may need comforting words from others, who will bring them joy to forget about their problems and believe that they will recover very soon.

Reference List

Cole, G. A. (1993). *Management theory and practice* (4th ed.). DP Publications.

Stanton, N. (2009). *Mastering communication* (5th ed.). Palgrave Macmillan.

Fowler, H. W., & Fowler, F. G. (1964). *The Concise Oxford Dictionary* (5th ed.). Oxford University Press.

Tull, A., & Coward, A. (2009). *Caribbean food and nutrition for CSEC*. Oxford University Press.

About the Author

There are some days when Geary Reid is excited to go to work, and there are other days when his excitement for working vanishes. Not all leaders will make employees feel that a workplace is an enjoyable place. However, in this literature, author Reid shares his knowledge and experience of working. He has worked with several organizations and at various levels. He wants to encourage persons that although they will go through many challenges as they work, they must look beyond those challenges, as there are many benefits for those who choose to work.

When Reid first started working, he did not recognize that there are benefits for employees. When he talked with other employees about work, many of them saw work only as something to occupy their time and to earn some honest money. However, Reid has seen many employees construct their own houses, purchase vehicles, and even send their children to school from the benefits they received while working. Many persons who are depressed attend work, become excited about their work, and find joy. Therefore, Geary Reid knows that work cannot only be seen as a bad thing but also as something important for those who like to work.

Reid tries to motivate employees every day, since he does not know what challenges they may experience at home. He believes that if employees are motivated, they will be more likely to have a mindset to do their best for their employers.

Many persons can establish good friendships at their workplaces. Some employees can even find companions as they work. Therefore, Reid wonders why some persons will only see the bad sides to being employed.

Over his years of working, Reid has developed many of his skills. He has been sent to many seminars by his employers. He has also represented his employers at both the private sector and government levels.

When author Reid first started working, he was not proficient with the use of computers and office equipment, but today, his skills have developed and he has trained many persons to use computers and software. As he works daily, he allows other employees to share their experiences and problems with him, and he shares his own experiences and solutions with them in return. He likes to see employees being successful, and he will hold the hands of many persons so that they can become better than he is, since he is not in a competition with anyone, but wants everyone to become great and to help their organizations to grow.

This page is intentionally left blank

This page is intentionally left blank

57

This page is intentionally left blank

58

This page is intentionally left blank

59

This page is intentionally left blank

This page is intentionally left blank

This page is intentionally left blank

62

This page is intentionally left blank

This page is intentionally left blank

64

This page is intentionally left blank

This page is intentionally left blank

This page is intentionally left blank

This page is intentionally left blank

9 789768 305657